CENZONTLE/ MOCKINGBIRD

Songs of Empowerment
(Poetry * Drama)

by Daniel García Ordaz

CENZONTLE/
MOCKINGBIRD
Songs of Empowerment
(Poetry * Drama)

by Daniel García Ordaz

FlowerSong Books

McAllen, Texas

García Ordaz, Daniel.
Cenzontle/Mockingbird : Songs of Empowerment : poetry, drama / by Daniel García Ordaz. – 1st ed.

ISBN-10: 0-692-07752-9
ISBN-13: 978-0-692-07752-8

Cover Art/Illustration by Mario Godínez
Published by FlowerSong Books: McAllen TX USA

Printed in the United States of America.

DEDICATION

To Maya Angelou and Gloria E. Anzaldúa, to Langston Hughes and Pablo Neruda, to Lorca and Whitman and Lazarus and Frost and Dickens and Dickinson. To Roberto Gómez Bolaños (Chespirito) and Eduardo Manzano y Enrique Cuenca (Los Polivoces.) Your words linger in me as I loiter in yours. To Lloyd Alexander for being my home base. To Walter Wangerin, Jr. for helping me see the possibilities.

Dedicated to my grandmothers, Abuelita Fina and Abuelita Chuy, whose voices still sing in my heart. To my wife, Gina, my kids, Anna, Laura, and Joshua. To my late father, Macedonio García, Sr., my mom, Rosa María Ordaz vda. de García, and my brothers and sisters (Max, George, Marco, Arturo, Alfredo, Martha, Gloria, and Felix), and to my tías and tíos and primos, whose voices I undoubtedly share, as I share with you my faith, hope, love, and sense of humor. Of thee I sing.

To the brilliant poets of the Rio Grande Valley International Poetry Festival with whom I've shared the stage or the writing workshop table or classroom.

To Dahlia, Dandy, Frank, Jessa, Victor, and volunteers at Art That Heals, and VIPF. To those who encouraged and guided me academically and in my writing career: Dr. Nikola Petkovic, Dr. Adelle Mery, Dr. Rebecca Jones, Dr. Sarah Neitzel, Dr. Rob Johnson, Dr. Phil Zwerling, Emmy Pérez, José Skinner, Dr. Rene Saldaña, Jr., Dr. Debbie Cole, Dr. Robert Lonard, Dr. Raymond Welch, Dr. Shawn Thompson, Dr. Amy Cummins, and George Gause and Virginia Haynie Gause.

To my amazing friends, artists, powerful poets, and muses of art, activism, strength, courage, and compassion: Jen Mendoza and Michael Jones and Katie Hoerth (who gave me excellent feedback), and to Edward Vidaurre, Veronica Sandoval, a.k.a. Lady Mariposa, Erika Garza-Johnson, a.k.a. Poeta Power, Amalia Ortiz, Amado Balderas, Jesse G. Herrera, Trev The Road Poet, Eddie Vega, One Deep, George Longoria, Marisol Campos, Lauren Espinoza, Katie LaMoine Martin, Veronica Solís, Lina Suárez, Linda Romero, Odilia Galván Rodríguez, Olivia Gatwood, Brenda Nettles Riojas, David Bowles, and Jan Seale.

To my fellow MFA in Creative Writing compatriots and comrades: David Jay, Lucinda Zamora Wiley, David Rice, Rosa Ledesma Treviño, Sarah Owen, LonAnthony Phillip Parker, Julieta Corpus, Isaac Chavarria, and Rodney Gómez.

To my fellow teachers and the great librarians and poetry and literary festival and writing workshop organizers who make the magic happen in ways we know and know not! Thank you, and "May you live to be a-thousand years!" (Joe vs. The Volcano).

To my students, past and present. May you be inspired. Thank you for inspiring me.

Cenzontle/Mockingbird

CONTENTS

AUTHOR'S PREFACE

Cenzontle/Mockingbird: Poetry As Empowerment

My collection is a polythetic assortment of poetry, lyrics, and drama that serves as a polyglottic exhibition of empowerment through mimicry. Like a mockingbird, whom the Aztecs call "cenzontle" in their Nahuatl tongue, my writer's voice is polyvoiced. I include in this collection an eclectic variety of voices: personas, languages, forms, styles, and identities—often mixing them, in part to entertain and in part to challenge my boundaries as a writer, to stretch my vocal chords, so to speak, but also in part to challenge the lingering prejudice against such *mestizaje*—or meeting and mixing of cultures (and also voices)—and help convert our society into one that accepts itself as it is: polyglossic and stronger for it. As Maya Angelou reminded us, indeed "We are more alike, my friends, than we are unalike." The sooner we embrace that truth, the sooner we can all join in the song that is America—the song that includes blues and jazz and *conjunto* and zydeco and yodeling and rap and bluegrass twang and *zapateadas*.

I approached the writing and the collecting, in part, as social criticism—as a necessary response to those prejudices that often pervade our attitudes around language and underlie interactions between and among the dominant class and Latinx, Hispanics, Chicanx, women, and other minority groups. I say "among" as well as "between" because some biases often pit, for example, Latino versus Latino—usually based on socio-economic status (evidenced by use of language and not by economic markers). How does a street-smart kid show up an uppity person with language? He can either out-street-talk him—rapper style—or he can school him with academic prowess—"Good Will Hunting" style. Through this collection, I engage both methods.

Ultimately, I wish for readers to acknowledge first that despite the recent evolution towards more welcoming attitudes regarding diversity in general and multilingualism in particular, writing in the U.S. is still generally expected to be produced in Standard American English. I wish for readers to acknowledge that I (and many like me) already appreciate and embrace texts by English-speaking writers of varying styles and voices; we simply seek some reciprocity. My collection is yet another invitation toward acceptance of linguistic diversity.

I use mimicry — in the kindest sense of the word — as a form of empowerment, not to crash the American party with an appetite for destruction, but for the sake of creating unity by celebrating the richness of American voices. Likewise, I invite the reader to mimic my work as tool of empowerment towards unity. My mentor and friend, Dr. Debbie Cole, a linguistic anthropologist, argues in her doctoral dissertation that performing "articulations of 'unity' using the familiar sounds of linguistic diversity enables ideological change . . . ." That is, "we can commit to recognizing diversity by sounding others' voices with our voices." In that vein, it is my sincere hope that the reader will recognize his or her voice in my writings and that the reader will "sound" my literary voice so that we may all be empowered to create unity through our diversity.

For the mockingbird, the ultimate goal is not to mock or mimic or even to show off. The ultimate goal in his sounding off in diverse voices is to gain a mate — to attract a female with which to unite and create a new and lasting relationship. America has more than one voice and more than one song. The contents of my collection serve as a reflection of that truth, of which I here sing.

INTRODUCTION

Now I Know Why The Poet Writes
Michael Jones
McAllen, Texas

The first time I ever encountered Daniel García Ordaz's poetry was during a FESTIBA reading at the University of Texas Pan Am in 2007. He had read a satirical poem entitled *Hot Out Here For A Pimp* about gardening under the balmy Valley sun; the title was ripe with the promise of being dirty and indeed its subject ended up getting dirty. Everything about the reading charmed me, especially that Daniel kept to the musicality of the source material — Three 6 Mafia's Oscar winning *Hard Out Here For A Pimp* — without directly attempting or mocking the Rap form. More than a mere reading of the poem, it was a *verbal performance* that seemed to exist in a place between singing and recitation. The performance was clever and well-executed, which should not be surprising, after all he is also known as The Poet Mariachi — a title that hearkens back beyond Mexican culture to the ancient Greeks, for whom music and poetry were inseparable. In ancient Greece, the poet and the musician were often one and the same person. And why does anyone write poetry but because of the natural music in his or her soul? When we're listening to the music of Stevie Wonder or Leonard Cohen aren't we also experiencing their lyrics as poetry? Shakira claimed that her two main sources on using the English language lyrically were Bob Dylan and Walt Whitman, and more than one critic has likened Eminem's Rap style to Shakespeare's poetics. Even Maya Angelou is best known for knowing why a caged bird *sings*. We ask so much of the music and poetry in our lives to help us tap into those intangible parts of reality … to shape our feelings … to console, to commemorate, to celebrate…. Poetry and music both help us navigate the more secreted depths of our inner worlds.

Reading poetry can be a deeply moving and unforgettable experience, and attempting to explain it can fall short of the profundity of that experience. When discussing poetry, it is easy to retreat into erudition, cultural or historical context, biographical minutia and political theory — to succumb to pedantry. Theories and evaluations can be interesting, even illuminating, but never as intriguing or profoundly layered as the poems themselves. It is always challenging to write something revealing not only about what happens within a poem but also within each of us reading poetry. My signature poetic experience happened in New York City in the early '90s, when, in an attempt to woo an Italian lover, I taught myself to translate into English verse the poem *L'Infinito* by his favorite poet, Giacomo Leopardi, that I would be able to recite it with comprehension in Italian — of course with my lover's guidance in pronunciation. To this day, the only Italian I can speak is the content of that poem and *"Ciao bello."* That is what poetry is supposed to do, transport us to a world that we can only understand when we are there, despite how little we understand of that world at large.

Reading poetry is an experience of incommensurability — at one moment a poem is deeply understood yet still not completely. Poetry offers an experience of meaning while withholding clarity and what fails to be articulated or captured with specific words can be compensated by a natural musicality of the language that will help the reader tap into what should at least be felt. Words are not always successfully communicated but music often is, and it is at that point that a good poet can seduce us when his verse eludes us ... this is why we are given to speak loftily of *composing* a poem rather than bemoan the drudgery of writing one, because *composition* best expresses the roles that sound and rhythm play in creating the poetic.

When discussing **Cenzontle/Mockingbird**, it would be the easy route to talk about classical poetic forms and jazz and mariachi music—that would be expected, an attempt to elevate a modern poet's words by linking them to established high minded cultural norms ... to give those words value by equating them with what we all agree is "great." Wouldn't we expect any astute critic of Langston Hughes' work to invoke jazz references ad nauseum? When I was asked to consider offering an introduction for this collection, that is exactly what I wanted to do; I also thought this was my opportunity to show off how culturally in touch I am with Latino/Chicano culture as an outsider. I had planned to write about *decimas*, a complex form of poetic verse that only exists in Spanish; invented in 1591 by Vicente Gómez Martínez-Espinel, a poet and musician from Spain's Golden Age. Espinel also added the fifth string to what we would eventually come to know as the Spanish guitar.... The *decima* crossed over to the Americas just like the Spanish guitar, and although we have lost Espinel's *decima* meter, his contribution to the Spanish guitar remains—and as such the soul of Espinel, therefore the soul too of his meter. The *decima* died about two centuries ago, but in the Latin Americas, forms of the stanza still thrive in some popular traditions. Particularly in Mexico, it survived as the *son jarocho*. But alas none of that is explicitly present in **Cenzontle/Mockingbird**; I was just trying to make some obscure cultural connection with the poet's nationality when what I needed to do was make a connection with his work.

At first I felt alienated from the text as it is not surprisingly saturated in colloquial Spanish peculiar to the border region that culturally knits the United States with Mexico. (Although I have lived in the heart of the Rio Grande Valley since 2006, I am still far removed from *la cultura de la frontera*.) While reading Daniel's collection, I would keep stopping and looking up this or that meaning, interrupting the rhythmic experience of the verse. I finally resigned myself to reading with my eyes metaphorically closed and stopped worrying that I couldn't mentally image some of the content ... I didn't know what some of the words meant but I at least knew how they should sound. I had to listen to what the sounds were doing and ask myself *"What do you hear Michael Jones?"* Sometimes we hear music voluntarily, when we choose to turn on the radio or play a CD and abruptly charm the air, manipulate moods . . . at other times we hear it deep inside of us, a private rhythm will strike our souls like a flash of lightning. This internal musical revelation is poetry already stirring within us, eager to erupt its own personal song. And when we listen closely to this inner music, the natural poetry of each individual identity becomes more complex and diverse; the infinity of who we each are begins to unfurl and each soul rolls out like a red carpet plush with ancestors stretching to forever. It is very important to know about our roots and from where we hail in history, but also to remember that we too erupt phenomenally like music from nowhere and are suddenly alive everywhere. To echo Ezra Pound, there is no end to the things of the heart, it is best to look and *listen*. It is the natural music of language intermingling with the music of the soul that is essential to the appeal and power of poetry. So I listened to Daniel's **Mockingbird**.

"What did you hear Michael Jones?" I heard Daniel sing the 'booty' electric in **Ode To The Nalgas** and **Los Nalgazos Cafe**, that he *likes big butts and cannot lie* ... I heard in **Famous**, Daniel chastising Bowie's man of **Fame** who's hard to swallow and promised no tomorrow ... I heard the ballads to all the beautiful girls in the world. I heard requiem masses throughout **Songs of Mourning**, for all the innocents

dead here and abroad ... I heard the sirens singing in forked tongues, beckoning me to crash against the eternal. I heard odes to joy and the spirituals sang out in the fields under an unforgiving sun. I heard all the music of the spheres. I realized that I did not have to confine myself to only listen for mariachi or corrido or Pedro Infante or Vicente Fernández because I was hearing all music and all singers ... every voice lifted bellowing 400 songs at once.

The *concrete* (or pattern) religious poems comprising **Songs Of Praise** expose another side of the Poet Mariachi ... the poet-as-singer is here a sage become architect, painter. Concrete poetry is an arrangement of words whose typographical effect is integral to conveying the poem's meaning. Everyone is acquainted with poet-speak terms such as *form* and *meter* and *structure*, but I wager most of us ignore the terminological connection to architecture and the fine arts. It is already a given that poetry has a painterly quality, that words are used in a way comparable to the abstractness of how the strokes of a painting come together to convey an image, but we rarely acknowledge that the poet has built an actual structure for the reader to explore level by level. Imagine a cathedral designed by an architect with a genius for painting the interior's frescos and even composing the masses that will be performed therein — that is the poetic splendor throughout **Songs Of Praise**. Like a modern Michelangelo of words, Daniel adopts the classical form inherited from the Greeks while evoking the iconic spirit of Robert Herrick and George Herbert and Guillaume Apollinaire. The definite and abstract designs of each verse speak to their respective subjects as well as collectively compose a kind of meta-music with shapes, much like the artwork of Vassily Kandinsky. This symphonic interlude is made all the more poignant by the middle poem, **Time Is Manna**, which hits three perfect notes right at its center: Time ... is ... Love.

It would be wrong to imply that the language barrier in any way hindered my experience reading *Cenzontle/Mockingbird* . . . if anything it was enhanced. I had to read it first for the music, then for the language and finally for the poetry. It took me back to my childhood lessons on reading Shakespearean drama—first time to learn the language, second the poetics, then at last for the play — lessons that served me well throughout this collection, which culminates in an ambitious reworking of the party scene from Act 1 of **Romeo & Juliet**. My initial reading of **Romeo & Juliet ¿Y qué?** I liken to a modern reader's challenging first encounter with Shakespearean English, as this drama is composed in English and Spanish, textured with Tex-Mex and *Caló* colloquialisms. (Chicano *Caló*, also referred to as *Pachuco*, has a combination of linguistic influences that include Hispanicized English, as well as Anglicized and 15th Century Spanish.) Even after sitting in on a private roundtable reading and discussion of the piece, when revisited on my own, I was again lost in translation . . . a matter ironically fixed not by sitting down with the text and a Spanish/English dictionary but side by side with the source itself, Shakespeare. What I understood about the original tragedy was brought to bear on my experience with Daniel's retelling . . . what I could not decipher I could still feel.

"Who are you to be a poet?"--a question rhetorically asked in **To the Poets, To Make Much of Rhyme** and perhaps privately asked by those souls bold enough to take pen in hand, regarding their own efforts. What does go on in a poet's mind and heart that leads him to create? What are a poet's materials by which he is properly endowed by nature to embark on such whimsy? Considering the poet of **Cenzontle/Mockingbird**, it is an inner music and intense response to life, a decorative spirit and a love for metaphor. Poetry comes to him in a flash of revelation, a flash of

response like lightning or falling in love. It is an event in his consciousness, a celebration of experience . . . the poet becomes aware that a particular form or shaping has imposed itself on the substance of words and images of his conscious state, yet are driven by internal sounds and rhythms happening at deeper levels of consciousness—those places closer to the soul. The composing of poems involves tension and interplay between various dynamics—singing, reverie, dreaming—all of which exist on that elusive plain between rational and irrational states of being. Much of what contributes to any poet's power is that he fiercely and fearlessly traverses this plain between reason and emotion and dares to tempt the eternal.

Daniel García Ordaz is a poet and a singer, but also a journalist and teacher . . . that he allows the conventional poise of the latter roles to be shaken—that his soul be stirred—is what makes him more than a man who simply writes poems, but rather a personification of the *poetic*.

Now I know why poets write, that everyone can hear their inner songs.

Lift Every Voice and Sing

"Words mean more than what is set down on paper. It takes the human voice to infuse them with shades of deeper meaning."
~ Maya Angelou

Cenzontle*

"Mockingbirds don't do one thing but make music for us to enjoy . . . but sing their hearts out for us. That's why it's a sin to kill a mockingbird."

~Harper Lee, To Kill a Mockingbird

And what makes a mockingbird special, anyway?
Why it's the trill from her tongue,
the cry from her lungs,
the sway of her lips,
it's her dusty, rusty, crusty cries,
the trail of tears in her eyes
on sheet music playin',
floatin' and swayin'
to the beat, beat, beating, way-laying,
saxopholaying,
assaulted, accosted, bushwhacked and busted,
cracked open, bruised, banged and accused,
flat broke and broken terror bespoken—
a token of survivin',
of thrivin', of juke joint jump jivin'
of death cheaten daily through unwanton wailin'.

Why a mockingbird's got diamonds
at the souls of her blues,
whip-lashed back-beats
at the edge of her grooves,
croons of healing above strangely-fruited plains of grieving.
She lets loose veracity with chirps
still rising at the edge of a knockabout life,
troubled and toiled
beat-boxed, embroiled,
de-plumed, defaced, ignored, encased,
caged and debased 'cause of the color of her skin.

But as the din fades and the cool of eve rolls in,
there she stands — chest huff-puffed and proud,
unbowed and loud, endowed
with the power of flight,
under the big dip of night,
echoing the ancient *Even* cry of a lioness
defending her pride
in that sweet mother tongue:
I rise up, and, *Adam,*
I shall not be moved today!

The mockingbird sings what the heart cannot pray.
The mockingbird sings what the heart cannot pray.

*Cenzontle is the Nahuatl (Aztec) word for the

northern mockingbird, *Mimus polyglottos.*

Soy Aphrodite ¿Y Qué?
(For Choral Voices)

I was spawned from the foam of fornication,
Brought forth from the gonadic sea,
Born from castrated emasculation,
Procreated to be   like me.
Rising exposed from a shell, like a pill-box invitation,
I am the cause of and cure for your sexual obfuscation,
The rhythm and rhyme of your heart's permutation.
I don't seek your approval or accept your affirmation.

I am the nightmare that you sic on your enemies,
The dream that you wish on your friends:
I am a hairy-armpit *greñuda*.
Soy Neruda *panochuda*.
I spit rhymes like a pissed-off *corajuda*.
I rip heads off like a praying mantis *viuda*.
Soy fuckin' hot and spicy like a bottle of *Cholula* —
Raw,   unrefined.   *Cruda.   Desnuda.*

Unprocessed.   Pure.   Young, but *madura*.
I don't need a dude, and I don't have a *duda*.
I'm a *chica   suertuda*, a *chica   piernuda*.
A lass with a snake-tongue, a *ruka venenuda*.
I be   killing you softly with my song
Like a mermaid in Bermuda.
You can get lost in my love triangle *que está super peluda*.
I'll exfoliate your cheeks and then leave you *bien jetúd@*.

I'm a coy mistress killa. A virgin *quebrantura*.
Soy chonguda,   trenzuda,   a short-haired *ruka-duda*.
I shall not be defined. I'm a stubborn *cabezuda*.

Soy leóna peleonera like a lioness of Judah.
I got truth   on lock   like an iron *cerradura*.
My conspiracies abound like a slow-motion Zapruder.
I'm a better good-luck-charm than a big-fat laughing
    Buddha.

I'm a *ruka   pachuca. Trucha   marucha.*
I give orgasms to the poor 'cause I live that kind of *vida*.
I kill swans and save Ledas.   *Heridas.   Queridas.*
Muchachas   perdidas.
We speak-yell-scream-and-shout, and we don't stay
    dormidas.

Soy mandona.   Matona.   Madonna   chingona.
Sangrona.   Enojona.   Nalgona.   Chichona.
Muchachona   fregada.   Castrada   arrastrada.
I give the world a *cachetada   al estilo* Lysistrata.
I knock truth   on its ass   *gacho-bad   a la Chingada.*

A Las Lenguas, Que Sigan Sus Cantos

A veces le decimos adiós a nuestro language.
En vez de tacos en la calle
Nos fijamos a ver que hay en el re-fridge.
No sé si entre este río
Habrá un suficiente land bridge
Para conectar los dos lados
De nuestra cultural heritage
Y a nuestros hijos poder cantarles
El viejo message
En el lenguaje salvaje
De nuestro mestizaje.

> *¡Qué viva México!*
> *¡Qué viva México!*

Que aunque suba nuestro American *aprendizaje,*
Que el México en nosotros no se baje.
Quédense, lenguas, calientitas
Como el té de canela
De nuestras abuelitas,
Como el caldo tlalpeño
De nuestras madrecitas.
Y no se pongan, lenguas, tibias.
Sigan cantando el viejo mensaje
En el lenguaje salvaje
De nuestro mestizaje.

> *¡Qué viva México!*
> *¡Qué viva México!*

¡Quita de tus platos ese sándwich!
¡Y enséñate a comer el viejo language!

Sin Labels/*Sin* Labials
(para Gloria E. Anzaldúa)

We are not born
With ideas about
Nationality
Language
Ethnicity
Religion
Gender
Class

Pero somewhere along the way
The powerful tend
To shovel that excrement
On the powerless

Make people walk around
With the kind of heavy baggage
Our enslaved forebears carried

Lessons quickly learned:
Classify or be classified!
Living or dead,
We taxonomize or die!

Here lies Gloria Evangelina Anzaldúa . . .
Nationality: *Tejana-Americana*
Language: Tex-Mexican-American, or Spanglish (*en Califas,
Nueva York, y Chicago*)
Ethnicity: Mexican American, *Chicana*
Religion: Pre-Columbian *Americaníndia Católica (con Sapphos)*
Gender: *Mujer*
Class: from *Pobre* to Blue Collar Scholar

Classification: *Mestiza, Chicana, Zurda, Aflijida, Chingada*

Sexual Preference: Woman On Top *y Mujer* On Bottom
Temperament: *Anzalduende*

Denaturalized
Dark-skinned
Demonized
Dismissed
Discarded
Denuded
Desolate
Described *de todo lo negativo* that can be thrown at a woman
who is
Desechable/disposable
Deemed *diferente*
Dissimilar
Divergent
Distinct
Diverse
Inderecha   But

Straight
lines are an abstraction of mathematicians,
those curved philosophers of logic.
Toda linea tiene curva.
All the earth is curved, circular, round.
Even the horizon
must bend to the laws of nature
not of man.

Yet we burn
      we yearn
      we turn

On each other we
Categorize we
Classify we

Label we
Sort we
Stereotype we
Pigeonhole we

Think we
Have the right
To don God's apron
And rename
What remains
From the clay
That he cools
On his heavenly stools.   But

We are not born
    To be   called.
We are just born
    To   be.

Our Serpent Tongue

Your *Pedro Infante*cide stops here.
There shall be no mending of the fence.

You set this bridge called my back
yard ablaze with partition, division
labelization, *fronterization*
y otras pendejadas de
alienization

Yo soy Tejan@
México-American@
Chican@ Chingad@
Pagan@-*Christian@*

Pelad@ Fregad@

I flick the slit
at the tip of my tongue
con orgullo

knowing

que when a fork drops, *es que ¡Ahí viene visita!*

a woman is coming
a woman with cunning
a woman *sin hombre* with a forked tongue is running
her mouth – *¡hocicona! ¡fregona!* –
a serpent-tongued *¡chingona!* with linguistic cunning
a cunning linguist
turning her broken token of your colonization
into healing

y pa' decir la verdad

You are not my equal
You cannot speak like me
You will not speak for me

My dreams are not your dreams
My voice is not your voice

You yell, "Oh, dear Lord!"
in your dreams.
I scream *"A la Chingada!"*
in my nightmares

Your *Pedro Infante*cide stops here.
There shall be no mending of the fence.

Songs of (In A Sense) An Experience

"A bird doesn't sing because it has an answer. It sings because it has a song."
~ Maya Angelou

To the Poets, To Make Much of Rhyme

You say you're a poet
'Cause you know
How to rhyme
All the time
Pantomime
Share your mind
Hit the stage
Show your rage
Be a sage
Despite your young age.

He will tell you to

Stop it!

when you
Emulate Neruda's style,
Walk a mile in Frost-ed flakes,
Shape your quips with Maya's guile,
Light a little dream of Langston's fuse,
Yaup with Whitman for a while,
Paint your muse in blue Plath hues.

He'll ask,

Who are you to be a poet?

As if poetry must be licensed and controlled.
He'll say,
Poetry is a luxury.
As if poetry is made of white-hot platinum gold.
A commodity of high society.
Untouchable.
Unteachable.
Unreachable.

But the fact remains that poetry is only for the bold.
To be a poet is to share truth.

To withhold knowledge is for the brute.
To be a poet is to be a conscious voice —
To rise above the pleasant noise.

We pledge allegiance to the math and science in order to
survive.
But if we really want to be alive — to thrive —
We must learn to dive into the deep end of the pool —
Leave behind the idea of being cool:
Embrace shame!   failure!   fear!
Run naked on the street.
Play with words that refuse to let us sleep.
Mold our words with passion and desire.
Dare to write as if our heart's on fire . . . .

So when he asks,

                                    Who are you to be a poet?

I say,
Who is he to even ask?
You're the one who stepped boldly to the mic.
He's the one still sitting on his ass.

Famous
(After Sekou The Misfit)

Has anyone seen my fifteen minutes of fame?
I just set them down for a minute
And things just don't seem the same.

Okay I know that sounds kind of lame

But, naw, see, I was famous once, yo!
Shoot, I was like the next biggest thing
On YouTube.
For, like almost a whole week!

Man, I have done it all for the camera!
I've smoked ten cigarettes through each nostril in my nose
and
I went water skiing once on the lake without my clothes and
Last week I ran through the mall with my momma's panty
hose
Around my face.
I even had my boy spray me with Mace!

On purpose.

While the cameras were rolling.

See, if you really wanna be famous
that's just the kind of sacrifice you have to make.
'Cause when you're surfing on top of a van goin' like 30
miles an hour
You'd better believe
You only get one take.

That's how I broke two ribs and got this limp.
People are, like,

"Dude, did you really break your legs
Or're you just trying to be a pimp?"

But, nah, I'll be a'ight.
I'm just waiting for Hollywood to call.
Naw, seriously though. Naw, for real, I'm fixin' to have it all,
     y'all!
Cars and money and things and . . . stuff.

I'm talkin' 'bout movie roles and real expensive clothes,
And my own mansion filled with Hostess Cupcakes.
Shoot, I'm 'a have my own island on my own sea
You know, just until they name a planet after me.

'Cause as long as the camera's rolling live and on the air
I'll do anything that most people wouldn't dare,
I'll be so famous people have to stop and stare.
Talkin' 'bout, "Damn! That dude's so famous it ain't even
fair.!"
Man, I'll be livin' larger than a Grizzly bear!
I can break every rule and the cops don't even care.
I'll have a posse of bodyguards around with four or five to
spare.
I'll even have a different girlfriend every morning with two
big breakfastses to share

Shoot, I'ma have my very own designer underwear
And my own brand of jeans.
And five television screens
in each bathroom.
So I can watch the news.
'Cause I can't read.
But, you know, at least I'll be "famous."

* * *

If you really want to be the star of your generation
Put the camera down,
And get yourself a college education.

Frida y Sus Sueños

*The bus driver got lost and arrived instead at a place in ruins
somewhere in México — surreal México.
The México that exists in dreams?
~Julieta Corpus*

The bus driver got lost and arrived
Arrived instead at a place
A place in ruins
A place somewhere in *México* — surreal *México,*
The *México* that exists
In dreams.

In dreams about masks and death
Deathly ill Frida and her *changos*
Changos with sunflowers and blue skies
Blue skies bloodied with red parrots.

Red parrots attacking your skin
Your skin peeling away like molten lava
Molten lava swallowing the moon
The moon shining on skulls on murals.

The bus driver got lost and arrived
Arrived instead at a place
A place in dreams about masks and death
Deathly ill Frida and her *changos*

Her *changos* attacking your skin
Your skin peeling away like molten lava
Molten lava that exists only in surreal *México*
Surreal México bloodied with blue skies
Blue skies and the moon shining on skulls on murals
The moon shining on skulls in dreams.

Unforbitten Love

I never dreamed that I'd be kissing you.
Star-crossed lovers often never meet.
Alas, I know that's why our love was blue.

The Fates told Cupid I was overdue.
I placed the Golden Apple at your feet.
I never dreamed that I'd be kissing you.

The bell struck twelve. I never found your shoe.
I stared at stairs and my heart lost a beat.
Alas, I know that's why our love was blue.

Love at first bite did change my point of view.
True love's first taste, they say, is bloody sweet.
I never dreamed that I'd be kissing you.

In Paradise our love was bare and true.
You let me taste your fruit that brought the heat.
Alas, I know that's why our love was blue.

My tresses locked the secret that I kept.
Your loving beauty cut them as I slept.
I never dreamed that I'd be kissing you.
Alas, I know that's why our love was blue.

Love Forbitten

I always dreamed that I'd be kissing you.
I begged for Night to come and bring my meat.
I'll never know just why our love turned blue.

I launched a-thousand ships as our love grew.
The horse, my groom, (our doom) the Fates did mete.
I always dreamed that I'd be kissing you.

The bell struck twelve. I'd hoped you'd found my shoe.
The heart of man is easy to defeat.
I'll never know just why our love turned blue.

Life's blood's a sweet bouquet when stakes are few.
In love, entombed in darkness, death we cheat.
I always dreamed that I'd be kissing you.

When Eden's serpent truth with lies imbued
The blame you laid, like thorns, upon my feet.
I'll never know just why our love turned blue.

My beauty learned the secret that you fibbed.
You tore asunder pillars as you lived.
I always dreamed that I'd be kissing you.
I'll never know just why our love turned blue.

Songs of In Her Beauty

"You alone are enough.
You have nothing to prove
to anybody."
~Maya Angelou

She

She was like a piece of cake.

Like the last piece of cake.

Like that corner piece of cake we all claim
with our eyes, feel entitled to in our minds,
long for in our hearts — some pining and praying shyly,
some publicly sharing our intentions
That tiny slice of heaven only one may obtain —
The one everyone assumes is spoken-for
Yet sometimes sits untaken.

She was like the winner of that last piece of cake,
Her sweetness sweetened by the victory
of the epiphany that she was not at all enough
but rather much beyond enough — that she wasn't
full of the fluff and superfluity of the frosting of beauty
but of substance and of layers and of hidden surprises in her
heart.

Beautiful Girls

Beautiful Girls is hard to spell.
Beautiful Girls are hard to tell.
Beautiful Girls aren't made of flowers,
Beautiful Girls are made of powers:
They can leap into your heart with a single smile,
Strong enough to bring guys to their knees,
Make us say "God bless you," when they sneeze.

Beautiful Girls are
Your best friend, so you don't wanna risk it

Beautiful Girls are
The worst enemies to be had:
They look so good that it's hard to be mad.

Beautiful Girls are
The sugar in my coffee,
The gravy that I sop up with a biscuit,
Three big scoops of Chunky Monkey ice cream on a
    chocolate-dipped waffle cone with
    whipped cream and sprinkles on top — and you don't
    have to share with your cousin!

Beautiful Girls
Can put a chink on a soldier's armor,
Can take the stink off a pig farmer.
They know how to turn on the charm.
They know how to warm up the barn.

Beautiful Girls are
The ones that said, "No way!"
The ones that got away,
The thorn at my side,
The times that I lied.

The reasons I cried.

Beautiful Girls are
The needle in my haystack,
The only reason I ever make my bed,
The curves on my guitar,
The 99 bottles of beer on the bar,
Soft rain on roses in June,
The top 27 songs on iTunes,

Beautiful Girls are
What makes a man crazy,
What keeps a man sane.

Beautiful Girls are
Staying up late, then sleeping 'til noon,
The tears from the man in the moon,
Sharing an umbrella in the rain,
The real cause of all my pain.

Beautiful Girls can
Part a busy sidewalk
Without words;
Turn noisy walkers
Into silent gawkers.

Jaw-droppin',
Eye-poppin',
Heart-stoppin',
Beautiful Girls can turn
Grackles into green jays,
Wayward weeds into bountiful bouquets,
Troublesome waters into tropical waves,
Old bald spots into new toupees,
Nightmares into holidays.

Beautiful Girls can turn
Winter snow into summer days.

Beautiful Girls
Make flatulence seem like potpourri sprays,
Turn a tiny spark into a raging blaze.

Beautiful Girls can
Turn a frown into a grin,
Make an angel turn to sin,
Make an atheist pray again,
Make you aks 'em, "How you doin'?"

Beautiful Girls can
Pay a waiter with a smile,
Make a long day's work last just a little while,
Make a cross-country trip feel like just a mile.

Beautiful Girls are sure enough
To make boys and men do stupid stuff:
Beautiful Girls
Make Humpty Dumpty get off that wall
(Fat boy was just tryin' to get a little somethin', y'all)
They make Yankee Doodle ride a pony,
Make a Muslim eat bologna,
Serve protein fanatics macaroni,
Make the DJs change their beats,
Make the butchers give up meats,
Make vegetarians skip the beets,
Make boys with no rhythm move their feets.

Beautiful Girls
Can make the Devil to repent,
Cause the Pope to give up Lent,

Beautiful Girls can
Get a cop to join the mob,
Make a mobster get a job,
Make you curl up your toes,
Take a knee and then propose.

A Beautiful Girl
Will wait to have a new name and a ring
Before she gives up the one Beautiful thing
That everybody knows Beautiful Boys are really after:
The love in her heart, forever after.

Le Finestre, or In Which My Lover Threatens To Throw Me Out The Window

If you throw me out the window
On the morning after we
I hope you take pleasure in exfoliating hugs
because I will gladly gulp down that glassy breakfast with
glee,
let it burn down my throat and churn inside my belly.

I will clamber crags and hillsides, brave the thorny
hackberry guarding your bedroom,
arrive just after dinnertime —
hungry, bleeding internally, excreting
silicone, soda ash, and limestone
through sandpaper skin reflecting the luminescence
of your scorching furnace.

Just to see you again,
I would daily peregrinate on hands and knees over newly-
broken bottles —
walk straight into your loving arms
and melt into your colored pane.

Coming (To The Point)

What up, ladies? I am a nice guy. Yeah. I know what they say. They say, "Nice guys finish last," but, see, I just want to make you come.

To a poetry slam.
At a coffee shop. At a library. At a bar.

I want to make you come so bad. On multiple occasions. I want to make you come early. Stay late. Sit in the front row. Don't hesitate. Make you glow. Make you the star of the show. And heck yeah, you can bring a friend to watch or jump on in. The water's fine. I don't bite, though my words will leave a literary mark, 'cause my words are mightier than my bark.

I want to make you snap your fingers. Nod your head. Sway to the scantily-clad beats of my metric feet. Move your soul. Move your mind. Move your behind in my figurative kitchen. Girl, I'm on a metaphoric mission!

I want to make you raise your hands to heaven in agreement or even hiss and shake your fist in disagreement. 'Cause I respect you. And I'm not intimidated by your intellect and ability to choose!

But when you do come, be prepared to have your nice-guy paradigm shift. And when you do come, be prepared to ride the naked crescendo of the curvy climax in my plot-driven stories and poems.

See, I want to make you sound your barbaric yaup! I want to make you come prepared to shout "Hallelujah!" and "Amen!" Shout gritos of spontaneous effervescent joy!

> In fact, I wanna hear you scream . . . like a first-year nun
> who hasn't forgotten
> how a cardinal sin is begotten!

> I wanna hear you scream . . . like a retard-
> ed fart that is louder than it would've been
> if it hadn't been held in!

I straight up just want to make you come. To the realization. That "ladies first" is not just a saying—it's a promise I will keep because nice guys do finish last! At poetry slams!

Oda de Odiseo a la Sirena

¿Dónde estás?

Ayer te busqué,
te hallé,
te perdí.

Hoy te buscaré otra vez.

Anoche te busque en mis brazos,
tan fuera de alcance como
la bicicleta de mi niñez —
hace mucho abandonada, jamás olvidada.

Te busqué en el eterno rugir
de tus caricias marinas
sobre las rocas
de mis memorias.

Remo y remo sin cesar
hasta que el latir en mi pecho
cae triste y silencioso,
débil sobre tu ancho mar.

Anoche escuché tu canto
en los vientos del verdor,
en los aires rumorosos sobre el abismo azul
suspiros que iluminaron mi paladar
con sabor a tí.

Extraño los murmullos
que dejaste como un eco dormilón
en el hueco de mi corazón.

Me dejaste como navegante sin estrella,
vagando hacia el horizonte gris,
extraviado, aislado, abandonado.

Ayer te busqué,
te hallé,
te perdí

Hoy te buscaré otra vez
aunque sigas enviando
tus olas de besos a dioses lejanos
chocando saludos
como holas de adiós.

Ode Of Odysseus To The Siren
(a translation by Daniel García Ordaz)

Where are you?

Yesterday I sought you,
I found you
I lost you.

Today I shall seek you again.

Last night I sought you in my arms
as far from my reach as
the bicycle of my childhood —
long ago abandoned, never forgotten.

I looked for you in the eternal roar
of your marine caresses
over the rocks
of my memories.

I row and row incessantly
Until the beating in my chest
Falls sad and silent,
Debilitated over your wide sea.

Last night I heard your song
in the winds of the green,
in the gossiping airs over the blue abyss
sighs that illuminated my palate
with flavor of you.

I miss the murmurs
that you left like a sleepy echo
in the hollow of my heart.

You left me as a starless navigator,
wandering toward the gray horizon,
lost, isolated, abandoned.
Yesterday I searched for you,
I found you,
I lost you

Today I shall look for you again
even as you keep sending
waves of kisses to distant gods,
greetings crashing
like waves of hello/goodbye.

Grapefruit Triptych

La Toronja

The flirtatious grapefruit
Blushes, ripe and round.
Wedged inside,
Her pink flesh hides
A bitter veil.

Her yellow shell,
Now broken,
Reveals white underpants.
Her daughters, desperate to be set free,
Escape into an ocean of sour waves.

La Toronja Japonesa

Flirtatious grapefruit.
Blushing yellow rind. Bitter
veil hides pink flesh.

La Toronja Hay(na)küensa

flirtatious
grapefruit blushing
behind white veil

Songs of Merriment and Exaltation

"In the struggle lies the joy."
~Maya Angelou

En La Pulga

"Quiero que me entierren/en Wal-Mart.
Es lo que van a hacer. Es lo que van a hacer.
Para que mi honey me venga a ver."
~Wally Gonzales, The Short-Legged Texan

A "new" pair of sneakers
The latest full features
The parking's free, *ya vente!*

A '94 Nissan
Pero sin transmichian
Your Tío Frank can fix it

St. Patrick's Day lights
Some Clinton/Gore kites
A wrist-watch/television

En la pulga se halla, se compra, se vende
¡Lo que pide la gente!

Aquí tienen Legos
Carritos y juegos
I want a *spiropapa*

Aguacates, nopales
Te llenan morrales
Con fruits *y* vegetales

Llantas pa' tus trailes
Los domingos hay bailes
Te ponen windshield wipers

En la pulga se halla, se compra, se vende
¡Lo que pide la gente!

Yo quiero gorditas
Arroz y carnitas
Frijoles a la charra

Taquitos al gusto
Te curan del susto
La lady *da sobadas*

Un hotdog *con todo*
Si me muero, ni modo
*También venden *coronas*

En la pulga se halla, se compra, se vende
¡Lo que pide la gente!

En la pulga se halla, se compra, se vende
¡Lo que pide la gente!

*funeral wreaths

Ode To The Nalgas

Round, curvaceous Amalgamation
All-encompassing, all-consuming
Firebrand of Inspiration

Geminal Butte
Cloned Colossus

Agitator-In-Chief
Plump Warrior

Stout, firm, solid corpulent mass of fleshy adoration
Mover, shaker, mischief maker

Pampered Pillow
Flatulent Fiend
Olympic Cushion
Icon of ill-repute
Seat of Perfection
Samson's deadly Weapon
Soft, smooth, supple sensation
Tough and tufted Tantalizer
Mountain of Desire
Fire

Clean-up: Table Five

One night at eight as we ate chicken soup
She had me pay for dinner, like a dupe —
This, after breaking up with me in front
Of strangers at a crowded restaurant.
To add insult to injury she asked
For me to drive her home that night and laughed
In glory at her triumph over love.
My heart, it stood — a loaded dove
Now caged, now maimed, now shot out recklessly
Against the door of opportunity.
I shall be telling this along with sighs —
I miss the road diverged between her thighs.
Though ne'er did love a heart as true as mine.
She was replaced a quarter after nine.

Some Like It Hot

Me encantan los pechos de mi novia Lucía
Que me presenta en cueros junto al cilantro
Y tomate que pizqué al amanecer el día
Pero no es por nada lo que dicen por allí —
"A esa mujer le gusta el chile."

Cuando me invita a cenar
Su mano quisiera pedirle
Pero después me pongo a pensar
"¡No'ombre esta mujer te quiere embrujar!"

Me arde tan feo por dentro
Que talvez de soltero estaría más contento.
Pero está tan bonita que no la puedo olvidar.
Piel morena y ojos negros tan profundos come el mar.
Ya la hubiera pedido si no fuera por su mentado paladar.

Nada más con verla se me para el corazón
No solo por su belleza, pero por el mismo calor
Y ya no se me baja el latir
Hasta muy después de meterse el sol.

Soy hombre humilde que bajo diario de los cerros
No le puedo ofrecer más que maíz, arroz, y frijoles
Y unos que otros becerros.
Hay cada cuando le doy un chile ancho y unos huevos
    rancheros.

Al fin, prefiero una señorita picosita a una que no sabe ni
    que es el sazón.
Pero hay les pido su bendición.
Porque para serle fiel,
Voy a tener que comer mucha miel.

Los Nalgazos Café

Do you ever wonder what would've happened if, instead of making friends with Bubba from Alabama, Forrest Gump would have agreed to go into business with Chuy, the *caníbal* from San Benito?

Welcome to Los Nalgazos Café

"We always enjoy having you for dinner."

The Body Part of the Month is . . . your ass!

We Can

Barbecued it, Boil it, Broil it, Bake it, Sautee it, Smoke it . . .

There's

Nalga Kabob	*Nalga* Soufflé
Nalga Gumbo	Sautéed *Nalga*
Nalga Creole	Pan-Fried *Nalga*
Deep-Fried *Nalga*	Stir-Fried *Nalga*
Pineapple *Nalga*	Lemon *Nalga*
Pepper *Nalga*	Coconut *Nalga*
Nalga Stew	*Nalga* Salad
Nalga Po' Boys	*Nalga* Burgers

The

Specialties of the House

Include

Nalgitas con Papas   *Asado de Nalga*

Nalgas Reynosa   *Nalgas en Salsa Verde*

Nalgas Cordon Bleu   *Nalgas* Foster

Sweet & Sour *Nalgas*

Nalga Guisada (con beans & rice)

Nalgas Flameadas   *Nalgas Piratas*

Nalgas on the Half Shell   *Coctél de Nalgas*

Nalgas Suizas   *Nalgas en Mole*

Nalgas a la Cubana con Plátano Maduro

Nalgas Poblanas

Machacado con Nalgas

Nalgas a la Charra

And, of course, for Vegetarians,

Nalgas Tofu

In honor of Lent

This Week's

Manager's Special

Is

The *Nalgóndigas* Platter.

The

~Nalga Du Jour~

Is

Nalga al Mojo de Ajo.

Los

Nalgazos Café

"It's a household name, 'cause like Chuy always said, 'There's nothing like a good piece of ass for dinner'."

Cafecito
(parody of "Despacito")

Sí,
sabes que ya llevo un friegos esperandote
Tengo que wake up *contigo hoy*

Vi,
the pot is empty *y estaba enojandome*
If you drink the last cup rinse it, yo!

Tú, tú eres el jarabe que quiero probar
Me voy acercando para el counter man
This line is too long *y eso no es justo* (Oh no)

I, I can't wait to hold you in my burning hand
Now my little heart is beating really fast.
Esto hay que tomármelo oscuro y puro

CA-FE-CITO
Quiero respirar tu aroma sabrocito
Men like Juan Valdez *te piscan despacito*
Con canela, crema, o bien sencillito

CA-FE-CITO
La dulce amargura de un Cubanito
Negro, azucarado, y bien calientito
Mexican, Columbian, *Americanito*

(Gimme, gimme, gimme! Gimme, gimme, gimme!)

I wanna see you roasted up
I wanna hear you grindin'
I want you to wake up my taste buds
So they're no longer deaf and blinded

I wanna spill your beans
I wanna feel you steamin'
I want your coffee pot to wake me
From the nightmare I been dreamin'

I know Starbucks be milkin' it
I know e'rybody thinkin' it
Starbucks makin' a killin'
'Cause chumps like us be willin'

I know I can save some money, baby — dumb, dumb
I know my bank account be wiggin', baby — dumb, dumb

I came up to the Dark Side knowing that it's evil
You don't have to judge me 'cause this stuff is legal
I got issues, Baby, I know I got baggage!
I try to drink it slow, but then I get all savage!

Espre-, espressito coffee *tan dulcito*
I'm getting addicted slowly, *al poquito*
When you kiss my lips like sweet cappuccino
You're making me an offer like I'm Al Pacino

Espre-, espressito coffee *tan dulcito*
We're getting together, like *un* puzzle-*sito*
Gives me an excuse to have some *pastelito*
It's the only way to eat some *pan dulcito!*

CA-FE-CITO
Quiero respirar tu aroma sabrocito
Men like Juan Valdez *te piscan despacito*
Con canela, crema, o bien sencillito

CA-FE-CITO
La dulce amargura de un Folgerito
Negro, azucarado, y bien calientito

French, Arabian, Swiss, or Indonesian-*sito*

(Gimme, gimme, gimme! Gimme, gimme, gimme!)

I wanna see you roasting up
I wanna hear you grindin'
I want you to wake up my taste buds
So they're no longer deaf and blinded

I wanna spill your beans
I wanna feel you steamin'
I want your coffee pot to wake me
From the nightmare I've been dreamin'

CA-FE-CITO
Please don't talk to me until my first *traguito*
I like it cowboy style with some *tocinito*
Can I get an Amen?! Can I get a *grito?!*

Espre-espressito coffee *tan dulcito*
I'm getting addicted slowly, *al poquito*

I wanna see you roasting up
I wanna hear you grindin'

Espre-, espressito coffee *tan dulcito*
We're getting together, like un puzzle-*sito*

I want you to wake up my taste buds
So they're no longer deaf and blinded

Songs of Fight or Flight

"You may encounter many defeats, but you must
not be defeated. In fact, it may be necessary to
encounter the defeats so you can know who you
are, what you can rise from, how you can still
come out of it."
~ Maya Angelou

Immigrant Crossing

My father's feet
Carried the sesquicentennial stench of
Mexico, turned Texas, turned United States of America.

He labored in 24- and 48-hour shifts
Irrigating arid citrus groves,
Working under the bellies of navel orchards
In trenches that emanated a stink
That America could not stomach.

Mother Nature painted on my father's immigrant feet
Socks of earth, wind, and tire,
Then drowned them in her melting pot,

Ankles aching,
Bunions burning,
Blisters bleeding,
Calluses calcificating,
Nails embedded with myriad funguses
Frolicking frivolously
Only to become penitent parasites.

My father left
Mexticacán, Jalisco —
Less than a spec
On the Mexican map —
And crossed the *Rio Grande*
For the privilege of standing on American soil,
For the privilege of owning an American acre,
For the privilege of raising his American children,
For the privilege of ruling
Over endless, waveless American ditches
For the privilege of working for
Endless, thankless *sanavabiches*.

On toasty Texas summer nights
When he'd come home at dawn,
We knew he was home upon smell,
As he shed his black boots
With a sigh of repose,
Crossing his feet
Under Uncle Sam's nose.

La Labor: Migrantes del Valle

I woke daily to the sound of my mother's wooden *palote*
gliding over the kitchen counter, where she flattened
the hand-kneaded dough to make flour *tortillas.*

Beans and *tortillas. Tortillas con* beans. Beans *con frijoles.*
Tacos wrapped in foil paper to keep them warm,
Wrapped in foil to keep away dust, bugs, hunger.

We dressed in long-sleeved shirts and hats, and raced
the sun through curving forest roads and drove.

Sometimes, *Tío Rico* would stop to fire at a deer
no one else saw from his window. And we drove.

We picked tiny cucumbers for pickling —
their thorny fuzz befriending our skin —
in a clumsy squatted waltz in the fog through endless rows
of green and dirt and sun.

We picked asparagus. Cleaned rows between potato plants,
radishes.
We picked banana peppers. Packed potatoes. And drove.
Our fingers smelled of dirt and pesticides.
There was no bathroom in the fields.

The day never ended.

All summer was one day and every day was workday.
'Apá would dip our sodas in a cold creek.
We worked and couldn't wait for lunch time —
at 10 a.m.

Once, with nothing else to eat in sight,
Nena and I devoured saltine crackers dipped in chocolate

frosting.
I was eight.

We'd get back to camp and eat and shower and sleep and
begin again.

Sometimes George would catch frogs at the canal before
dinner.
Sometimes *Arturo* would run with *Licha* from Edinburg,
who was in Cross Country and had nice legs.

The few Sundays when we didn't work all day we played
baseball.
Mom hit a homerun.
Dad played cards until two in the morning.
Marco was his good-luck charm.
Tío Rico danced with a goat on dad's birthday —
and then cooked it.

Minnesota. Wisconsin. Arkansas. Texas.

I hated interstate truck stops
with lights like a surgeon's lamp
that startled us awake.
I feared the spaghetti crisscross highways,
the tall overpasses of the big cities.

One year, on our way home, our station wagon burned.
The engine overheated. The grass caught fire.
Mom saved a blanket she was knitting.
The ball of yarn rolled out of the car, aflame.
My mother prayed about it.
My father wrote a song.
Tío Rico cursed.
The kids cried.
Max's fishing rods melted to the car.

Half of what we'd earned burned
with that avocado green station wagon
We moved on.

We were split up and got a ride to the next migrant camp
from strangers.
A black trucker dropped off three of us in Hope.
I don't remember how we got home to Texas.

Back home, every season had its crop
Every Saturday its early start.
We picked onions and onions and onions and
cantaloupes and tomatoes and oranges and grapefruits
and onions.

When the teacher asked me to write about where we had
gone
during our summer "vacation"
I always said the same thing:

Nowhere.

El Muro: The New Colossus
(after Emma Lazarus)

Though data demands that I exist
My mathematics do not compute
Programmed to divide
Instead I subtract

I keep the cats of prey encaged
I keep the flightless birds enslaved
I give no life
I am ashamed

No songs I raise
No water flows
I block the ways
I seal the door

I find solace in the sighs of the wind
Caressing my iron beaded seams
I find mercy in the beating sun
Tanning my hide, my dying dreams

I cry no peals of joy at church
Nor *slip the surly bonds of earth*
I sail no fair-wind open sea
I live to kill
In infamy

Not a bridge
Not a tower
Not a soul
Just a briar

I hide my lamp
Beside the golden door

Since those like you
Aren't welcome anymore.

In America*

technology has evolved
racist people have not

superimposed images on maps
they created of lands they did not

real people have also appeared
on this continent

 a regular paradise
in the Land of the Gorch

with no puppeteer in sight
no papers

only their underwear and hopes—
the Electric Mayhem continues

*(a found poem from an article about Jim Henson's Muppets
   and Sesame Street. Italicized words are from the article.)

In-A-God, A-New-Vita

Poor wretch. It refused team in shores.
Why people want to come here, I don't know.
Crashing mosaic fluttering destiny,
Ramp and in dull gent strangers energized by time

Why people want to come here? I don't! No!
Instinctive double-cross of oceans leaves. Love's behind.
Rampant indulgent strangers, energized, buy time.
Into one another we must feed.

Instinctive doubt. Crossing ocean leaves loves behind.
Hunt and gather luggage, gun, and blanket.
In two, one.   Another we must feed.
Compass, compact Bible, community.

Hunt and gather lug. Gauge gun and blank it.
Faceless names on tiered family trees.
Come. Pass. Come, packed Bible. Come, Unity.
Genetic disconnection—planned in retrospect.

Face less names.   On, tired family trees!
Foreign heirs air different goals.
Genetic disc connection planned in retro specs.
Poor: wretched refuse teaming shores.

Your Own, Personal Coatlicue: Blues Do Be A Mockingbird

"Music was my refuge. I could crawl into the space between the notes and curl my back to loneliness."
~ Maya Angelou

Just Selfies
(For Vincent)

What wondrous strokes we might behold.
What enchanted lights and curves and swirls
upon a woman's naked bosom or smooth, bent back.
The artist's loving hand turned flowers into gold,
self-portraits filled with agony untold,
abandoned streets of old into romantic
boulevards of broken screams.
But Van Gogh's night scenes starred no starlets.
Painted ladies don't jut out from his canvases.
Gaugin offered no large nudes on loan.
What they don't tell you about Vincent
is that his brushes stroked no hips.
What they don't dare mention
is the violence and the fits.
What they don't like to talk about
is the depression and the ticks.
Crazy doesn't sell until the paint is dry
and the body has been tagged.

But You Don't Date Guys Like That

He wants to love you

like a death row inmate loves
    the sun, the pain of knowing

like suicide bombers love
    martyrdom, the smell of burning flesh

like a butterfly loves
    nectar, the caress of the wind

like America loves
    Chipotle, cultural appropriation

like Juárez loves
    tequila, butchering women

like Austin loves
    food trucks, gentrification

like Chicago loves
    deep-dish pizza, murder

like *Los Angeles* loves
    itself.

He would miss you like

a metaphor misses like, or as

a racist misses George Wallace, or as

the sand dunes miss the waves, or as

71

a new mother misses the weight, or as

a bullet misses   the dark, still
smell inside a fully-loaded gun
under a motel pillow.

He's The Man

Sweet salty sweat lingers long on his petrified lips
forever stained with guilt and the conviction — again —
that this must never happen again —
until next time duty falls
and the curtain calls
on the dry heat of Afghani desert knights.

Golden wedding rings don't ring true
when soldiers exchange foreign American flesh
in foreign landscapes. Vows are set aside
like long-forgotten memories of run-down lots
in corners of dying towns where oil's been discovered.

In the morning, the light of Sunday sun sears sinner's skin —
a lover's tan from slivered sun through wrinkled curtains
made of aluminum foil and pizza boxes sent frozen
by wives praying for safe returns.
Her task of dressing for Mass made difficult
by shared uniforms to match the shared breathing
reminiscent of a first college love.

In the morning, the dream will end
and she'll walk alone to her barracks
with no explanation for her absent snores.
He'll get a knowing nod
from the private on duty last night
for the extra hump witnessed on his mattress.

At church that morning,
the chaplain will speak of the woman caught
in an adulterous affair
who would be stoned.

(No mention of the man.)

My Dearest Nadine
(inspired by the film "Drugstore Cowboy")

I want to carry you
In my arms and steal you away
Throw you over my shoulder
Drop you as gentle
As a pillowcase full of yesterday's downy dreams
Bury you in a light blue bag
In a perfectly rectangular pit
Dug deep within a green wood of pines and ferns
That smells of gleaming checkered floors in rundown
theaters
Mopped into forgetting the bloody stains of slit throats and
burst veins and ashes.

I want to take you for a scenic drive
Down a muddy back-road in Oregon
Lay you down where unseen birds will serenade you sweet
lullabies
Pat the earth smooth and cross myself and just walk away —
Away from spinning hats and blue skies and all —
Hop back on my old green truck
Shove off without a word
Like a drugstore cowboy
Forget about the whole thing
Drive off into the sun
Set my eyes on the fast-fading horizon
In the rearview mirror
And be good. Be a regular guy.

Tomorrow
(after Rankine)

Tomorrow I want a massage.
I want a deep, rough massage that deletes
memory like a virus on a poet's laptop.

I want the hurt of someone else's pissed off
ex-wife to come down on me —
like Holocaustic hurt.

A Mr. Spock shoulder-grip massage.
A sinfully scintillating Santa-girl massage.
Pretty, flirty, thirty-year-old pain.
Pain that left her feeling like discarded leftovers pain.

Pain that sore knuckles feel after beating
fists of wrath — bath-water rain drops
of sorrow for yesterday and today and
tomorrow never comes alive
and tomorrow never lived
or died.

Tomorrow never brings relief,
just pain tomorrow.

Pain like the longing for
escape a carousel horse must feel
at the promise that tomorrow
he'll be free.

But tomorrow,
pain.

Songs of Mourning

"No matter what happens,
or how bad it seems today,
life does go on,
and it will be better tomorrow."
~ Maya Angelou

A Time For Mourning

Time heals no wounds.

Pain never dies.

Time flies, and with it, pain little by little subsides, but there's no expiration date on pain and there's no term limit on mourning. Period.

It's not easy letting go, and it's absolutely not required.

Even when your heart is broken, the sun will rise, beautiful and pink and orange and purple and warm but the grief is not retired.

Morning leads to morning as mourning leads to mourning and the pain you thought was naught will come back without warning.

You'll cry for the moment. You'll cry for the memories.

Sadness will hit you in unexpected places on unexpected days:

on days when the sun is shining and when clouds fill the sky,

in the third inning of a baseball game and at halftime during football season,

when your son holds your hand in a parking lot, or when your daughter goes off to college.

Time heals no wounds.

Pain never dies.

Time flies, and with it, pain little by little subsides.

London: July 7, 2005

The Union Jack flew proudly in the breeze   at 8:51 in the
     morning.

They were on their way to work   at 8:51 in the morning.

The first bombs exploded   at 8:51 in the morning.

The underground tunnels shook   at 8:51 in the morning.

They didn't know what hit 'em   at 8:51 in the morning.

It was hard to breathe in the trains   at 8:51 in the morning.

The passengers cried out loud   at 8:51 in the morning.

The faces and the streets were bloody   at 8:51 in the
     morning.

They took pictures with their cell phones   at 8:51 in the
     morning.

The bobbies ran and the ambulances rolled   at 8:51 in the
     morning.

Nurses ran to help the wounded   at 8:51 in the morning.

They performed C.P.R. on the street   at 8:51 in the
     morning.

They pulled the dead from the trains   at 8:51 in the
     morning.

They prayed to God   at 8:51 in the morning.

The Pope blessed himself   at 8:51 in the morning.

They searched the debris for clues   at 8:51 in the morning.

The terrorists pissed me off   at 8:51 in the morning.

They shouted, "Bloody Bastards!"   at 8:51 in the morning.

The world got a little smaller   at 8:51 in the morning.

Strangers held each other close   at 8:51 in the morning.

The English roses wilted   at 8:51 in the morning.

The sun still kept rising   at 8:51 in the morning.

Deadlines: The Tragedy of Media-crity
(Sandy Hook: December 14, 2012)

They will rank you
They will Connecticut you down to palatable pieces of
　　footage
A-B-C-and-D-roll through your town
They will calculate and hope to see you
Make the top-five school massacres of all time —
Other countries need not apply —
They will synonymize you in perpetuity with Columbine,
　　Virginia Tech,
And some other third shooting they'll have to google

They will rank you
On a slow news day, they will thank you
For becoming the lead
Story after story after story
They will file you
They will roll up and down the town
And profile you
Run an exposé on every mother-father-sister-brother and
　　defile you
Interview your neighbor, your friend, your enemy, your dog
Salivate at the chance to out your every indiscretion
Make you the cause of the killer's transgression
Veil thin your every sin

They will rank you
They will list and classify and bank you —
The victims and the families
The survivors and fatalities
The heroes and the wannabes

They will rank you
They will heatedly discuss you

Over pictures, fonts, and headlines
They will credit and discredit you
Plaster your picture in the paper
Check Wikipedia for a connection to the date
Check Facebook profiles for tell-tale signs of hate

They will rank you
They will dramatize and victimize and sterilize you
Until the death-weary world retracts
Until the next celebrity drunk attacks
Until the next death do you part
Until the next anniversary
Then the five-and-ten-year mark

Autumn: Massacre In Paris
(Le 13 Novembre, 2015)

I.
Leaves change: fall.

II.
Leaves change fall.

III.
Fall change leaves.

IV.
Change leaves.
Fall.

V.
Fall leaves change.

VI.
Fall leaves.
Change.

VII.
Change.
Fall.
(Leaves.)

Songs of Praise

"Let gratitude be the pillow upon which you kneel
to say your nightly prayer. And let faith be the
bridge you build to overcome evil and welcome
good."
~Maya Angelou

Left-Centered, Right Justified

Leftists are communist pinkos.
Guerrilleros

Zurdos
Malcriados
Looking for a handout
Siniestro/Sinister/Wrong
Liberal global warming propagand*istas*
Leftistas barristas

Centrists are lukewarm.
Neither hot nor cold
Just fine for Goldilocks,
Not good enough for Martin
Como los hermaphrodites
Ni de aquí, ni de allá
Playing for both teams
Passive-Aggressive Reformist-Conservatives
Republicrats/Demopublicans
Philaphobes/Phobiaphiles
Che/Hitler Hybrids
"I voted for it
before I voted against it."
Peaceful Warriors
Seriously Funny
Simple Genius

Rightist are mightists
Under a conservative light
Kristallnacht/Crystal Night
Right to life/Right to bear arms
God and country

*Dextro/Derecho/*Right
Nazis *supremecistas*
Fascistas capitalistas

And e v e r y o n e f e e l s *t o t a l m e n t e* j u s t i f i e d .

Good thing God is *bien trucha con* Word!

Creation

in seven days God
made the universe divine
nature in its prime

Numbered Days

I see

    The crashing hours
        Upon the sands of time,

    The crested days and
        Weeks and waves
            Ending with a sigh,

        The roaring months
           And rolling years
              Waving their goodbye,
              Tossed in
            metronomic pace —

        Empty as they lie.
      And on that calm horizon
    Where God threw down His rock,
  Where tidal ripples started,
The end of time is nigh.

Time Is Manna

Time is a sustenance that cannot be hoarded.
The end of time will never be recorded.
Time soothes the aches that
come from great mistakes.
To spend time is a virtue.
To waste time is human.
To give time is divine.
Time can't be bought.
Time can't be sold.
Time is ever on
the horizon.
Time
is
Love.
Time has
No heir, no care,
Absolutely no despair.
Time is a harsh extorter.
Time is a gentle exhorter.
Time cannot be recreated.
Time cannot be destroyed.
Time is always never late.
Time is karma's incubator.
Time is the rarest jewel to behold.
Time is Manna, a providence of Heaven.

Bendición en el Sillón
*(Blessing on the Sofa)

Que fregado de mí	How miserable of me
Hoy yo amanecí	For today I awoke
Sin tortillas, sin pan, sin café.	Sans *tortillas*, sans bread,
sans coffee.	
A la calle salí	I took to the street
Casi de hambre morí	Almost starving to death
Y a la casa de empeño yo fui.	And straight to the pawn shop I went.
Puse en empeño	I pawned
A un jalapeño	A *jalapeño* pepper
Y un nicle me dio el señor.	And a nickel the man gave to me.
Con el nicle compre	the nickel I bought
un taco al pastor	a barbecue *taco*
Que sin chile no tenía sabor.	That, sans *chile*, much flavor lacked.
A la casa volví	To my house I returned
Y con gran frenesí	And with a great frenzy
De rodillas le ore al Señor,	On my knees I prayed to the Lord,
Y el Señor contesto,	And the Lord answered,
"¿No te he dicho que Yo	"Have I not said that I
Sere tu Proveedor?"	Shall be your Great
Provider?"	
En el viejo sillón	In the aged sofa
Me halle un tostón	I found a half-dollar piece
Y de pronto a la tienda corrí.	And then hurriedly ran

to the store.

Que dichoso de mí	How lucky of me
Ya que tengo aquí	Now that I have with me
Mis tortillas, mi pan, y mi fe.	My *tortillas*, my bread, and my faith.

*(Poem loosely translated from the original Spanish version to English by the author.)

Heaven Sent

Days of old
Prophets speak.
Babe foretold.
People seek.

Shepherds slept.　　　Angels sang.　　　Promise kept.
　　　　　　　　Behold the Lamb!
Virgin-born.　　　Wise Men seek.　　　Star-adorned.
　　　　　　　　Born so meek.
Dove soared.　　　Heaven sent.　　　Called the Lord.
　　　　　　　　Knees are bent.
Truth restored.　　　Folks repent.　　　Crowd adored.
　　　　　　　　Lame men leapt.

Demons warred.
Cup accept.
Crowd roared.
Mother wept.
Maimed and gored.
Christ crept.
Mocked and scorned.
Silence kept.
Nailed to board.

Skin torn.
Christ forgives.
Crown of thorns.
Thief lives.

God disowned.
Angels mourned.
Sin atoned.
Christ entombed.

Darkness ends.
Third day rose.
Christ ascends.
Living prose.

The Beginning and The End

In the End
    I will want nothing,
        for I shall have it all

In the End
    Everything I now own
        I shall never need again

In the End
    I will love perfectly
      and be
          wise,
            beautiful,
              holy,
                complete

In the End
    I shall be your child
      and you shall be my God,
      and therefore,

My Beginning

Encore: Dial "M" For Mexican

"Love is a condition so powerful; it may be that
which pulls the stars in the firmament. It may be
that which pushes and urges the blood in the veins.
Courage: you have to have courage to love
somebody because you risk
everything — everything."
~ Maya Angelou

ROMEO & JULIET *¿Y QUÉ?*

A Reimagined and Adapted Scene

In Chicano Caló, Tex-Mex,

Spanish, and English

ROMEO & JULIET ¿Y QUÉ?

A one-scene adaptation of Act I, Scene 5 of William Shakespeare's "Romeo & Juliet" reimagined as a contemporary *fiesta* attended by two competing cholo gang/families in an American Latino/Hispanic/Mexican American community.

Characters:

CAPULET: *El mero-mero chingón;* father of JULIET; 60

EL VIEJO CAPULET: Old-School *Cholo* in a zoot-suit; wears an Army Vietnam medal; 65+

LA JULIET: beautiful, young jail bait; *hija* de CAPULET; 13

TYBALT: lieutenant of CAPULET; *sobrino* by marriage; 18

ROMEO *MONTESCO*: handsome son of CAPULET's rival; 16

BENVOLIO: *primo* and best friend of ROMEO; 17

LA NURSE: Older lady; only woman wearing a dress or nightgown—with shawl; indigenous/bronze skin; 55

GUESTS--*VATOS LOCOS & CHICAS SUAVES*

VATOS LOCOS: Men of different ages — though mostly younger, mostly muscular, wearing well-dressed and pressed *cholo* attire; some wear zoot-suits (partial or full); some have their top button buttoned — but none other, and the shirt's untucked. Some have visible tattoos; aged 14 to 45

CHICAS SUAVES: Women of different ages, shapes, and sizes, dressed as cholas (no dresses) in t-shirts or muscle shirts, some with jeans and some with khakis, with *chola* eyebrows and make-up, including blue or pink eye-shadow. Some have tattoos; aged 15 to 45

LOS SERVINGMEN: Young muscular men wearing white muscle shirts, matching khaki pants, black suspenders, hair nets, and Stacey Adams shoes; aged 14 — 33

Setting:

Party at CAPULET's house. Evening.

Time:

The present.

Act I, Scene Five:

At Rise: CAPULET stands facing stage left, greeting the GUESTS (who spread out and mingle inaudibly throughout the stage after being greeted by CAPULET, who poses occasionally with GUESTS for a camera (flashing OFFSTAGE). CAPULET greets the *VATOS LOCOS* with a combination of handshakes and half-hugs and with bows and kissing of hands or kisses on the cheek for the *CHICAS SUAVES. LOS* SERVINGMEN pace hither-thither, some carrying serving trays and occasionally handing bottled beer to other GUESTS, JULIET, *LA* NURSE, and TYBALT, who are already inside the *fiesta*. Party music can be heard in the background. A *VATO LOCO* who's shirtless in the corner is cornering a *CHICA SUAVE*.

(Entran CAPULET, *EL VIEJO* CAPULET, *LA* JULIET, TYBALT, *LA* NURSE, *LOS* SERVINGMEN, and *todos los* GUESTS--*VATOS LOCOS & CHICAS SUAVES al pori*.)

CAPULET

¿Qué onda, Carnal?

(Poses for the camera with *VATO LOCO* and other GUESTS;

returns attention to others.)

Ey, Homes!

(Greets a *VATO LOCO*; resumes attention to others.)

¡Bienvenidos a todos! ¡Aquí están en su cantón, Ese!

(Poses for the camera with *VATO LOCO* and other GUESTS;

returns to others.)

Las chachitas que no tienen callos en sus dedos bailarán con

ustedes. 'Hora sí, mis jainas, ¿quién de ustedes se negará a

zapatear? Ajúa! El que no se ponga a tirar chancla, le diré a todo

mundo que tienen callos. ¿No que no, cabrones? ¡Órale!

¡Pónganse! ¡A bailar se ha dicho! 'Sup, carnal? *Nombre yo antes*

96

también me ponía a menear el bote, pero it's been a while,

Homes. *Yo hace un friegos que supe cómo hacerle pedo a las*

chavalónas. I could whisper some sweet something-

something in a honey's *oidito,* you know. *Pero, chale, Ese. Ese*

tiempo ya paso pa' mí. I'm too old for that! Ey, come in, *Carnal!*

¡Todos son welcome! Ey, deejay, *ponle, Carnal! ¡Haste garras!*

(Music plays, and they dance. To the SERVINGMEN)

¡Hagan campo! ¡Muevan ese pedo!

(To the *CHICAS SUAVES*)

¡Órale, rukas, shake those *nalgitas!*

(To *LOS* SERVINGMEN)

¡E, güey! ¡Más luz acá, baboso! ¡Limpien las mesas y muévanlas

pa' allá! ¡Y apaga esa lumbre! ¿No vez que 'ta muy hot? *¡Este*

vato!

(To his CAPULET CUZ)

¿Qué onda? ¡Primo! 'Ta con madre este pori, que no? ¡Nombre

siéntate, güey! ¡Hijuesú! ¡Ya 'tamos too old *pa' este pedo!*

(CAPULET and his COUSIN sit down)

¿Desde cuándo que no nos vemos en un borlo como este?

EL VIEJO CAPULET

Te lo juro que ya hace un treintón de años, Homes.

CAPULET

¡Chale, Cuz! *Nombre, ¡no mames! ¡No es pa' tanto! Wátchale: ¡la última vez fue en el* wedding *de Lucho! Yo sé que el tiempo pasa en friegas, pero son hace* 25 years ago, *¿qué no?*

EL VIEJO CAPULET

¡Nel pastel! Son más, ¡Primo! ¡Son más! ¡Al hijo de Lucho ya le cuelgan, Carnal! ¡Ya cumplió treinta años el dude!

CAPULET

¡A la mo! *¿En serio,* Homes? *¡Su hijo era un chavalón hace dos años!*

ROMEO

(To A SERVINGMAN)

Ey, *Vato, ¿quién es esa* chick *hablando con aquel* dude?

SERVINGMAN

Sepa la mo, *Carnal.*

ROMEO

Ssss. ¡Mamacita! ¡Da más luz que un cuete en el 4th of July! *No es de Dios. 'Ta demasiado buenona pa' esta vida!* Damn! That baby doll is too damn fine *pa' que la entierren cuando muera! 'Ta hecha pa' dar luz a las estrellas! ¡Se ve más puri que un* dove *entre cuervos! Cuando se acabe esta* song, *la wa seguir a ver que ondón. Hijuesú!* I never been *enamorado* like this! *Mis* eyes *me mintieron antes.* I never been in love *hasta 'horita!*

TYBALT

Que jodidos? Ey! I know that voice! *Este vato es un Montesco.*

(To his PAGE)

¡Tráeme mi daga, Ese!

(*Bien* angry.)

¿Qué jodidos hace aquí ese méndigo con su cara escondida en una mask? *¿Cómo se atreve el güey? ¡Me lo voy a destrampar pa' que se le quite!*

CAPULET

Ey, *quihúbole, Sobrinito?* Why you mad, Bro?

TYBALT

¡Tío, este vato es un Montesco — nuestro enemigo! ¡Es un canalla

que vino a fregar con nosotros aquí en tu chánte!

CAPULET

¿Ese dude *es el tal Romeo?*

TYBALT

¡Simón que sí, Tío! That's the *sanavabiche!*

CAPULET

¡Calmantes montes, Carnal-ation! *Tíralo al león y no te agüites.*

Dicen que este vato no es mala onda. I hear *que* he's actually a

pretty chill dude, T-Dog, so *no te esponjes,* Cuz. *No quiero pedo*

aquí en mi borlo, so ponte al alba y respétame, Homes. *Ponte las*

pilas y aliviánate, ¡¿okay?!

TYBALT

¡¿Cómo que no me voy a esponjar con ese canalla aquí, Tío?! He

shouldn't be here, ey! It's our party!

CAPULET

I already said *que* he can stay, Homes, so chill out, *Ese! ¡Ya* hablé! ¡¿Qué jodidos? ¡¿Aquí yo mando, que no?! ¡No seas

soflamero! ¡Si empiezas pedo con todo mundo it's gonna be your

fault, not mine! ¡No quiero bronca en mi cantón, Ese!

TYBALT

Yeah, but, . . . ¡Tío, . . . pos . . . he's disrespecting us!

CAPULET

¿Quién chinga'os te crées, huerco mocoso? Are you being for

real, Vato? ¿Te creés el mero mero fregón o qué? ¡Mira, Sobrinito,

ya te he dicho que conmigo se te nubla, cabrón! No me vuelvas a

rezongár or I will kick your ass right here in front of your

homies, ey!

(To los GUESTS)

¡Simón! Ta bien de aquellas, Carnal! That's bad ass, ey!

(To TYBALT)

¡¿Entonces que, güey? ¡Ponte trucha o te descuento! You hearing

me, fool?

(To los SERVINGMEN)

Hey, Fool, more light over here, Ese! 'Ta bien dark aquí!

(To TYBALT)

'*Che huerco mocoso sin vergüenza! ¡Te me callas el hocico y te me largas a la fregada,* or else, *Ese!* You feel me, Homes?

(to the GUESTS)

Órale, Ese! Échenle ganas, Carnal! ¡A bailar se ha dicho! Ajúa!

(*La música* continúes *y los* GUESTS *bailan.*)

TYBALT

¡Me tiembla el pinche cuerpo como perro enrabiado! ¡Me wa ir, ey, . . . *pero este pedo que por 'horita le parece bien* sweet *a Romeo le va* taste-*iar amargo al güey!* Laterz, Homes!

(*Se va el* TYBALT *bien* pissed off, all *sentido el* dude.)

ROMEO

(Takes JULIET's hand.)

Tu mano es como un holy place *que mi mano no debe tocar. Pero si te ofendes que te 'toy tochando con mi* hand, *pos mis* two lips *aquí están listitos como los* pilgrims *pa'* fix-*iarlo con un besito,* ¡ey!

JULIET

Cálmate, Homes. *¡No manches! Dale un poco de* credit *a tus*

manos. By holding my hand *me enseñas respeto, y, pos, al fin,*

los pilgrims *tochan las manos de las* statues *de los santitos, ¿qué*

no? Poniendo una palm *contra otra* palm *es como un besito, ¿ey?*

ROMEO

¿Qué no tienen los santitos y los pilgrims lips *también?*

JULIET

¡Simón, Ese! — pero esos lips *los usan los* pilgrims *pa' orar.*

ROMEO

Pues entonces 'ira, Santita: deja que tus lips *hagan lo que hacen*

tus hands. *'Toy orando que me des un besito. Dame mi oración pa'*

que no cambie mi fe por desesperación.

JULIET

Los santos no se hacen move, *ni hasta cuando conceden una*

oración.

ROMEO

Pos entonces no te hagas move *mientras tomo el efecto de mi*

oracioncita.

(*Le da un* kiss *a la* chick.)

¡*'Hora sí!* You took my sin *de mis* lips *con tus* lips.

JULIET

¡Híjole! ¿Y a poco tienen mis lips *el* sin *que te quitaron?*

ROMEO

¿El sin *de mis* lips? That's *firme! Me animas que sea un* smooth

criminal *con tu dulzura. ¡Regrésame mi* sin *pa' 'tras!*

(*Otro* Kiss.)

JULIET

Hijuesú! ¡Besas con madre!

NURSE

Ey, *¡Mi 'ja, te habla tu 'Amá!*

(JULIET *se va* to the side.)

ROMEO

¿Quién es su 'Amá?

NURSE

A lo mero macho, Hijo, su jefita es la mera señora del cantón. Es

bien de aquellas. Yo mismito le di pecho a su hija cuando estaba chiquitirrina. *Wátchate, deja te digo algo,* ey: *¡el vato* that

marries *esta rukita le va caér un diablaso de lana! Te digo que se*

va a rifar. ¡La mera neta, ey!

ROMEO

(To himself)

Más triste! Hijuesú! 'Toy bien salado! ¿Es Capuleta? ¡Me lleva

San Gaspar! ¡Mi vida loca is now in the hands *de mi enemiga*

chaparrita!

BENVOLIO

(To ROMEO)

¡Ponte trucha, Carnal! Vámonos antes de que se ponga malo este

pedo!

ROMEO

Simón, Ese. Ya se pone tristón este pedo.

CAPULET

¿Qué onda, muchachos? ¿Cómo que ya se van? ¡To'avía falta la

tragazón!

(They whisper in his ear *que* it's late, so *ya estufas — ya es muy tarde el pedo.)*

¡A la mo! Bueno pues, thank you for coming, ¿ey? *¡En serio, Carnalitos! ahí nos watchamos,* Homes. *Buenas noches a todo mundo. ¡Ya se me hizo tarde! ¡Alúcenme aquí! ¡No sean güeyes! Fuímonos al* night-night!

(To his COUSIN)

'*¡Hora sí, Primo!* Goodnight *porque ya se va metiendo la luna. ¡A dormir se ha dicho!*

VIEJO CAPULET

Como dice el dicho: Old *cholos* never die. They just go to sleep, *Carnal. Ahí nos watchamos,* Homes.

CAPULET

You said it, Homes. Buenas noches!

(Everyone except JULIET and *LA* NURSE begins to exit.)

JULIET

¡Eit! Psst! *¡Ven pa'aca! ¿Quién es ese vato firme?*

NURSE

¡Ese es el hijo de Tiburcio, el que tiene friegos de feria!

JULIET

No, ¿quién es el que se va saliendo 'horita? The one that's

leaving, *¿Ey?*

NURSE

Pos ése se me hace que es aquel pachuco El Flaco.

JULIET

¡Nombre, esta chick!! *¡Te sales! ¡Yo digo el que sigue de él!* The

one that *no quiso* dance!

NURSE

¿Pos quién sabe Tú?

JULIET

¡Con una chin . . . ! Go and ask! *¡'Juesú!*

(*Se va LA* NURSE chick *a preguntar.*)

¡Si está casado mejor muero en vez de casarme con un baboso!

NURSE

(Returning.)

Se llama por nombre Romeo. Pero ése cabrón es un Montesco y es

el único hijo de tu peor enemigo.

JULIET

(Talking to herself, *la* chick.)

¡A la fregada! ¡No lo puedo creer! ¡El único hombre que amo es el hijo del mismo diablo que odio! Lo vi demasiado temprano sin conocerlo, and now it's too late. *Qué babosada la mía. El amor qué enamora al enemigo es amor qué enamora sin sentido.*

NURSE

¡Ay, Dios mío! ¿Qué es lo que dices?

JULIET

Nombre no es nada más que un poemita que me enseño este dude *que* danced *conmigo.*

(Someone *del otro lado* calls, "Juliet!")

NURSE

¡Ya vamos, pues! ¡Vente, mi 'ja! All the *vatos locos ya se fueron.*

(They exit, *y se acabó el pedo* — for now.)

(END OF SCENE)

ACKNOWLEDGEMENTS

Grateful acknowledgement to the editors of the following journals and publications, where some of the following works have appeared.

I would also acknowledge those who've awarded my writing or included me as a guest or featured poet or keynote speaker at countless schools, clubs, and festivals.

Praxis Magazine Online: "Cenzontle"

Juventud! Growing up on the Border (VAO Publishing): "La Labor: Migrantes del Valle"

Poetry of Resistance: Voices For Social Justice (The University of Arizona Press): "Immigrant Crossing"

La Bloga Online Floricanto: "Our Serpent Tongue," "Immigrant Crossing," and "Oda de Odiseo a la Sirena"

Left Hand of the Father: "My Dearest Nadine"

Harbinger Asylum: "In-A-God, A-New-Vita" and "Tomorrow"

Interstice: "La Toronja," "Numbered Days," "En La Pulga," and "Creation"

Encore: Cultural Arts Source: "Frida y Sus Sueños"

100 Thousand Poets For Change: "*In America*"

Gallery: A Literary & Arts Magazine (UTRGV): "Romeo & Juliet ¿Y Qué?"

Texas Intercollegiate Press Association: 3rd Place: Spanish Story: "Romeo & Juliet ¿Y Qué?"

Caja de Resistencia: "Immigrant Crossing"

Resist Much/Obey Little: Inaugural Poems to the Resistance (Spuyten Duyvil Publishing): "Immigrant Crossing"

* * *

Border Book Bash

Dallas International Book Fair

FESTIBA

Gemini Ink Writers Conference

McAllen Book Festival

Texas Association for the Improvement of Reading

Texas Association of Bilingual Educators

Texas Book Festival

Texas Center For The Book

Texas Library Association

University of the Incarnate Word

UTRGV

ABOUT THE AUTHOR

Daniel García Ordaz is the founder of the Rio Grande Valley International Poetry Festival and the author of *You Know What I'm Sayin'?* (El Zarape Press, 2006) and *Cenzontle/Mockingbird: Songs of Empowerment* (FlowerSong Books, 2018). His focus is on the power of language, which he celebrates in his writings and talks. In April 2017, García Ordaz defended his thesis, Cenzontle/Mockingbird: Empowerment Through Mimicry, to complete his terminal degree, an MFA in Creative Writing from The University of Texas-Rio Grande Valley. Over the years, he has edited several books and anthologies, such as *Twenty: In Memoriam*, a response by poets across the U.S. to the Sandy Hook shootings.

García is a teacher and writer, and an emerging voice in American, Mexican American, Chicano, and Latino poetry. His work has appeared in numerous literary journals, academic collections, and anthologies. He was born in Houston in 1971 and raised in Mission, Texas. His publishing experience including editing and book cover design credits.

García also a song-writer, former newspaper journalist, photographicationisticator, and word-maker-upper. He appears in the documentary, "ALTAR: Cruzando fronteras/Building bridges" itself an altar offering to the late Chicana scholar and artist Gloria E. Anzaldúa, one of his great influences for this collection. García was one of five authors and the only poet chosen to participate in the Texas Latino Voices project in 2009 by the Texas Center For The Book, the state affiliate of the Library of Congress. He has been a featured reader and guest at numerous literary events, including the Texas Book Festival, the Dallas International Book Fair, McAllen Book Festival, Texas

Library Association events, TAIR, TABE, and Border Book Bash, among others.

García also served in the U.S. Navy as a Hospital Corpsman. He earned his Bachelor of Arts degree in English from The University of Texas-Pan American. He lives in the Rio Grande Valley of deep South Texas with his wife, Gina, and their children and he continues to teach write, sing, and spend time in front of a crowd as often as he can. García Ordaz is listed in Poets & Writers. See videos of him on YouTube and follow him at @poetmariachi. He may be reached at poetmariachi@gmail.com.

ABOUT THE COVER ARTIST

Mario Godínez, a.k.a "El Mago," was born in León Guanajuato México, but has been living in the Rio Grande Valley of deep S. Texas for more than 20 years. Godínez graduated from Harlingen High School South, where his art teacher encouraged him to pursue art. He then went on to receive his BFA from the University of Texas Pan American in 2008 and became a high school art teacher himself. He currently lives and works in his hometown of Harlingen. Godínez aims to inspire young artists to make their own contribution to the world. Both the pop art and the surrealist movement have influenced his work heavily, inspired by the everyday monsters such as stress, anxiety, depression, insecurity, and nervousness. Using art as a therapeutic weapon, Godínez creates in order to defeat his modern day monsters. Along the way he hopes to inspire many people with his creativity and continue to positively influence his students into becoming the best artisans they can be.

Follow his work at @elmagoart on Instagram and Facebook.

CPSIA information can be obtained
at www.ICGtesting.com
Printed in the USA
LVHW111359021118
595750LV00001B/274/P